Hues of The Rainbow

Written By

T.Oscar Whaley

Four Books in One

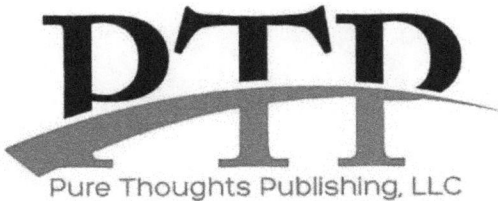

PTP

Pure Thoughts Publishing, LLC

Copyright

Hues of a Rainbow

Table of Contents

Hues of a Rainbow 9

Reflection of The Spirit 36

God Inspired 62

Inspirations

Dedicated to all that share in the love of
The Spoken Word. May you find as much
enjoyment as I did writing them.

Hues of a Rainbow

Vol. 1

PRAISE

For Today, Tomorrow And The Rest Of My Days,

I Will Always Take Time To Give God Praise!

When I Was Ready To Give Up Just Quit

He Calmed My Nerves, Made Me Just Sit.

To Think Of From Whence I Came

Since Accepting Him in My Life, It Hasn't Been The

Same.

So From Now On, Forever And Always

I Will Start My Day By Giving Him Praise!

ALL THE PARTICULARS

All The Particular, And So Much More

I'm Willing To Give, There's More In Store.

If Ever Anyone Deserves All These Things.

For Certain It's You, With Diamond Ring.

It's My Greatest Desire to Afford Them To You,

Because So Grand You Are

So I Pledge To Provide You, All The

Particulars…

WHEN WE'RE APART

There's emptiness I feel when we're apart,

It's as if there is a whole going straight through my

heart,

This really doesn't describe how I feel,

But I do know I feel ill.

Just the thought of not being with you, sends my world in

a daze.

You know I love you, in so many ways.

I've recognized this from the very start.

And I only feel it when we're apart.

HOW WILL I KNOW?

How will I know?

When the special person you've always

dreamed of

Is right before you, is it true love?

All you can think of is the next time you meet.

Just the thought of this makes life so sweet.

There's always a chance, which way do you go.

So tell me friend, how will I know?

Do I run away, for fear of being hurt, misused?

Please help me out; I'm just a little confused.

Is this real love, or just the show?

If I don't give it a try... how will I know?

FOR ONCE IN A LIFETIME

There has a place where I can go

A place to find myself does anyone know?

Where you can rest your burdens, take some time

out A place to exhale, to be yourself without any

doubts.

I know there has to be somewhere out there

Does anyone know, is there anyone who cares?

How do you go about finding this place?

Without fearing a slap in the face?

We all are in search of this place in time

To just for a little while, find peace of mind

Can there be a place of any kind

Where I can just be myself, for once in a lifetime?

The Extra Mile

If you really want to achieve your goals, then every

Once in a while there's one thing you must do, go the

Extra Mile.

How else do you fulfill your life's dream?

If you're never willing to rise as the cream

Which always find its way to the top

In your pursuit of excellence, you must never stop.

So whatever you do, do it with a smile.

It makes it much, easier going the extra mile

ACTIONS

Actions are the form of expressions when

Used the wrong way they can cause

depression

When used the right way, they can bring such joy

Like an excited child, with their favorite toy so

Think it over before you speak your mind

rehearse

Because once they are done it's hard to reverse

What's said in anger, may not be how you really feel

The one who hears it, believes it's real

Maybe you think this sounds absurd as I

Said before, think about the words

PATIENCE

Patient Is the Key to Overcoming Life's Game

Without It You Get All Of The Same.

Obstacles, Heartaches, and Frustrations It's True,

So Have Some Patience, It's All Up To You.

It Can Make a World of Difference on the Outcome

So Give It a Try, Go Ahead and Have Some

You'll Be Surprised at What Way You Think And Hear

What You Should See, Is Now Perfectly Clear?

Come On Now, This Has to Make Sense

You Have Nothing to Lose, So Have Some Patience

RARE

A Woman Like You Is Rare These Days,

You Are Such A Gift, In So Many Ways.

If Ever There Were A Person So Loving Warm And

True

There's No Doubt In My Mind It Has To Be You.

To Have the Pleasure of Knowing Someone Like

You

Comes Once In A Lifetime.

I'm Honored to Be the One, And To Know You're

Mine.

Even If Only For a While,

I'll Always Think Of You With A Smile

DIDN'T I?

When You Were Feeling Lonely And Needed A
Friend Didn't I?

After All The Pain And You Thought There Was No
End

Even Then, I loved You Through Thick And Thin
Didn't I?

I Promised To Always Be There For You
But I Make Mistakes, But Don't You

Somehow I Always Made It Up To You
Didn't I?

I'LL NEVER

Love Anyone As I've Loved You,

To Me There's No One Else For Me But You.

This Is What I've Waited A Lifetime For,
Someone Like You, Who I Could Adore.

If By Some Misfortune That I Should Lose You,

I'll Never Love Again, The Way I Love You.

HOW ABOUT US

You Want To Be Loved And So Do I
How About Us Giving It A Try?

We've Both Been Hurt One Time Too Many,
Between The Two Of Us We Have A Lot Of Love And
Plenty.

How About Us, Move Past Our Differences, And Give
Love A Try?
Who Else Understands Me And Who Understands
You?
On This We Agree For Sure It's True,
How About Us?

CONSIDER THIS

In Everyone's Life A Little Rain Must Fall

There's No Exception, Big Or Small

We All Have A Burden That We Must Bare

Life Is Tough, But It's Also Fair

You Win Some, You Lose Some Is A Familiar Verse

But Just Remember, It Could've Been Worse.

In Us All, There Is A Story

Then Too, We All Fall Short Of His Glory.

To Think Otherwise Is Just A Wish

Take A Little Time And Consider This...

ALMOST THERE

When Times Are Tough, Don't Give up You're Almost There

Just At the Moment When It Seems No One Cares

You're closer than You Think, Almost There

The Light at the End of the Tunnel Seems Miles Away

But You're Almost There: Today Could Be the Day

It's Easy To Just Throw In The Towel

Then Again It's Better To Tough It Out For A

While You Can Find Average Anytime or

Anywhere

So Excel To Be Your Best, You're Almost There

ESPECIALLY FOR YOU

All I Do Is Especially For You

If There Was More That Too, I Would Do

For You Have Brought Such Joy to My Life

Can't Wait For the Day That You Become My Wife

There Has Never Been Happier Soul Than Mine,

Simply Put You Are Truly Divine

Whatever It Is You Do, Please Don't Stop

I Know You and I Are On Our Way to the Top

All The Adversities Together We've Gone Through

So Forever I'll Give My All, Especially for You...

BELIEVE IT

I'm Sure You've Heard Them All Before

But Coming from Me It's For Sure

No One, Can Mean It As I Really Do

Just, Wait and See, I'll Prove It to You.

I've Never Wanted to Please Anyone- No Not Anyone

Yes, In Doing So For You, Seems Like So Much Fun.

Not In the Sense of Playing a Game

It's About The Way I Feel When I Speak Your Name.

Your Intelligence Precedes You, So I Know You Can Conceive
It

My Beloved It's True So Just Believe It

ABOVE ALL

You're The Closest to An Angel

That I've Ever Seen

Just Ask Anyone Who Knows You

They'll Know What I Mean

You Make Mistakes, but We All Do

Above All Else, Your Intentions Are True.

Even when you're Angry, You're Very Being Can

Be Seen

That's Why Above All, You My Queen

MY WILL OR THY WILL

I Have Some Questions I'd like To Ask Of You
Concerning Your Life Choices, And What You Do
Do You Handle Them Your Own Way, Is This True?
Or Do U Place Them In Hands Of Our Savior
Or Did You React, With An Irrational Behavior
Causing An Even Bigger, Situation
_Because You Reacted, With No Hesitation

My Will Or Thy Will
Have You Considered, Just Maybe, This Was A Time
When You Needed GOD?
Or Does This Sound Ridiculous, Maybe Even A Little
Odd
However In Hindsight, The Purpose Was To Reveal
Are Operating On
My Will Or Thy Will....

SISTERS

From The Time When We Were Kids

Remember All the Fun Things That We Did

Sometimes We Argued and Got Under Each Other Skin

But Then We Would Make Up and Start All Over Again

Even When We Were Determined To Not Even Speak

Sometimes This Went On For Days, or Maybe Even Weeks

However When It Was All Said and Done

I Wouldn't Trade You for Anything, Being Your Sister Has
Been So Much Fun

Not Only Are You My Sister but Also You Are My Friend

This Is the Bond That We Will Share Forever, One That Will
Never End

IF YOU EVER

If you ever need a friend

Count on me until the end

a shoulder to cry on, and a listening ear

I'll even be there to wipe away your tears

For in you I found what is truly rare

Someone who understands, someone who cares

Anytime is the right time I'm here for you

Whatever it is just ask, I'll see you through

So don't hesitate no not ever,

Because I'll be there, remember if you ever

SO CLOSE

We've come so far from hurt and pain,

So close to turn and run again

If not now then when do we?

Except that it's just you and me.

Together we're happier than we've ever been before

There's a whole lot of living for us in store

Let's make our union forever and complete

The thought of losing you is obsolete

We're so close don't turn back now

How could you consider it just how?

When were so close...

WITHIN

In all of us there is a burning desire,

To be successful, full of passion and fire.

Trying so desperately to be heard,

Although there are times when we can't find the words.

Yes, deep within, there's something and new,

And with faith and patience the way will shine through.

If you only believe, for it lies within you.

A GIFT FROM THE HEAVEN

You happened along, when I was troubled
and confused

A gift from heaven, how it all happened I am
amused.

Handpicked by God, and sent personally to
me

I'm better person with you in my life, with

You I want to spend eternity.

JUST FOR TODAY

Just for today, I will try to be all that l can be,

Facing the world and its many adversities

Just for the day I will take a chance

I will look at the big picture, not just take a glance

Seeing the world through my own eyes,

Taking it all in with no surprise.

Just for today, I will keep in mind,

That it doesn't come faster than one day at a time.

'Inspirational Poetry'

REFLECTION

Of The Spirit

T. Oscar Whaley

Reflection of The Spirit

Vol. 2

REFLECTIONS

As I woke up this morning about to start my day,

It dawned on me; how I've come a long way.

For not long ago I was lost and in despair,

No one to talk to, no one who cared,

But now I know, I was not alone

For it was God who carried me,

while sitting at His glorious throne

I have no doubt what He has done for me

All I have to do is reflect back, it's plain to see.

No longer do I worry about what tomorrow will bring

It's in His hands, so forever His praise I will sing.

What He's done for me, He can do for you,

Just open up your heart and let His love shine through.

He's always there with open arms,

To lift your spirit by His anointed charm.

If anyone out there knows what I'm talking about,

Then just say, Amen! Don't whisper it, shout!

YESTERDAY

As I open my eyes ready to face the new day,

I, for a moment, gave some thought to yesterday.

Whatever happened is in the past now,

Today gives you a chance to make a difference the
question is how?

You learn from the mistakes and the obstacles that get
in your way,
That's the benefit of looking at yesterday...

TURNING THE CORNER

As, I venture out into the world today,

I always take time out to stop and pray.

My life has been filled with trials and tribulations,

But also it's been filled with joy and celebrations

Today, I am blessed to know how far I came,

Enjoying each day, no two are the same.

Turning the corner........

A HERO LIES IN ME

There was once a time, when I settled for less

Not giving my all, refusing to give it my best

What difference does it make, who cares anyway

All the while, I was wasting myself, from day to
day

I look up and 20 yrs., have gone by

I wonder, what I would have become, I'll never
know, because I didn't even try

Then one day, it was as if GOD himself opened my
eyes

You can be whatever you want to be, don't you

realize

If you make up your mind, for it's never too late

So what are you waiting for, let's not
procrastinate

Set your goals, to where you can achieve them;
make them plain to see

For that's where I've come to believe that A
Hero Lies in Me.

IMAGINE

Imagine if you will a world with no trials and
tribulations

Image you and 1 on an extended vacation.

Just a star suspended in time,

So goes our love when you heart meets mine.

A walk in the park a long relaxing ride

Imagine you and I we'll take life in stride.

WITH YOU

When I'm with you, in good times or bad,

I realize we'll make it, it makes me feel glad.

Together or apart, I'm not alone.

With you, I have someone to call my own.

We're not perfect, on that we agree

But without you there's no me.

TRUST

If we're to make it, and have a real chance,

To weather the storm, dance the last dance.

Then, this my love is a definite must,

In each other we must trust.

We've both had our share of heartaches and
pain,

Trust is the key for our love to remain.

APPLE OF MY EYE

This is for that special someone,

Who comes along once in a lifetime

You're one in a million, truly divine;
You bring such happiness to all you meet,

To know you, is to love you because you're so
sweet.

How I came to be with you, I don't question why,

More importantly, you are the Apple of My Eye.

IN YOUR EYES

When I look in your eyes, I see promises, I see love

I see hope and trust just peaceful as a dove.

Your wisdom and your honesty are beyond compare

It's so nice to see, in your eyes you care.

MINE TO GIVE

If this world were mine to give,

I'd give it to you, so wherever you wanted you could live

In my possession, I would have all the treasures

I would bestow them upon you: even then it couldn't measure.

What I have to give and plenty of

Is the one thing you deserve, that thing call Love

ONE MINUTE

May I have a minute to express myself?
Right at this very moment, whilst my pride is
on the shelf
Now, I can stop, and take a long look at me
You know reflect back, on how I use to be
Always putting things in perspective, for
someone else to see
But never, using any of it, for me
As I listen to that voice, of reason in my
head
I fall to my knees, and thank GOD, that I'm
not dead
For little did I know, I was out of control
Not until being full of me, had taken its toll
Yes sixty seconds, is all that I need-
From this day forth, will I now, my own
advice take need!
For in these words I say, and its contents,
there is love in it
For all you really need is...

ONE MINUTE...

WHAT WOULD YO U DO?

If you knew that today was the day that our
savior would come

What Would You Do?

Or do you even believe in him and his return,
others, more than some

Truly believe, as the time is drawing near

That the one who died for us all will soon appear

Is your house in order, have you gave your life
for him?

Can you, without a doubt. lay down your life, or
will you follow them

You know them, the procrastinators, naysayers, and such

Never taking the time, to pray or repent, yet ask
him for so much

What Would you do?

When the sky split open, and there he is
descending down on a rolling cloud

If you haven't come to know HIM in his Kingdom
you won't be allowed

For he knew you not, but gave you every chance

By His stripes ye were healed, and by His mercy
forgiven every circumstance

How about that lie, you told, that dollar you
stole, or maybe even that heart you broke

Can you say this out loud, or on these words will
you choke

What Would You Do?

Are you hearing me feeling me or do you even care?

So many will be left behind, standing with a blank
stare

No sin is too big or too small to repent and ask for forgiveness

If you listen closely, there's a message in this

No man knoweth the day or the hour, if we only knew

If God was coming today

What Would You Do?

NEXT TIME

We all make mistakes it's just human nature

So let's not be so hard on ourselves, for it gets
better later

Perhaps, there may be some way to get on the
right track

They say trouble only last for a while, and that's
a fact

If only I had another chance, how many times do
we really need?

To realize it takes believing in yourself, in order
to succeed

Be true to thine own self, and lay it all on the line
For like it or not, right now is Next Time....

BLESSED

On the day I met you, I was truly blessed,

I tried to hide it, but oh, how I was stressed

But every time you came near my sense of
direction became vividly clear,

All the reason more, that I love you my
dear.

Blessed, is what I've been abundantly,

Surely, heaven's missing an angel because
you're right here with me...

AFTER THE RAIN

There's certain calmness, after the rain.

This I observed, while peering out the pane.

The air smells fresher; the sky's a soothing
blue,
add a rainbow to the background, what a
wonderful view!

It can be so relaxing, just sit and stare,

At the birds as they fly, so freely in the air.

After the rain, it's quiet, so serene and still.
Picture you and I together after the rain,

If you will!

THE CHOICE

We all have the choice, to decide what is wrong and
what is right,

There's no in between, you either stay in the dark or
come into the light.

It's all in your hands. So what will you do?

Use it wisely, when you make The Choice.

PRECIOUS

As rare as a gem, unknown to man

Giving love unselfishly, as only you can.

With such style and grace that can only come from heaven up above

You're the epitome of the word known as love.

To find such a gem is no small feat

Just having known you made my life complete.

A match made in heaven when god paired us

That is why you are so precious.

FOR ONCE

I'd like not worry why

Nothing goes right, no matter how I try.

There has to be a path that I can take

To right what is wrong, for goodness sake.

For once I just want to do what's right

At the end of the tunnel I see the light,

But how do I get there? Show me the way,
Are there words that I should say?

There are three words and you'll never be the same,
When you say them for once and believe

In Jesus' name...

I APPRECIATE YOU!

When days were cloudy, you are the silver lining

You know all the right things to say, without even trying.

You're as elegant as a Queen sitting on a throne,

Simply put you're the most wonderful person, I've ever known.

I appreciate you!

FAITH

In the worst of times, I remember to stand fast,

It may seem like forever but this, too, shall pass.

Even when I am down and in despair,

My faith never waivers for He's always there,

Of course, At times I wonder why things
happen to me, still
Then, I remember it's all part of Gods will.

IN TIME

In time, life brings about a new perspective,

What and how we choose to see it, is the objective.

We may never know the wonders of it all,

Just as the season change: winter, spring, summer and fall.

In good times or bad times, no riddles or rhymes,

Everything must change, but only...In Time.

'Inspirational Poetry'

GOD INSPIRED

T. Oscar Whaley

God Inspired

Vol 3

IS YOUR HOUSE IN ORDER

Can I, or should I say may I, ask this question of you
It's one that's quite personal, So to thine own self be
true

IS YOUR HOUSE IN ORDER

Have you, or are you operating on Thy Will or My Will be
done
This is an all-inclusive question, so it applies to everyone

IS YOUR HOUSE IN ORDER

I mean let's be serious, often times we all need a reality check
Otherwise, before we know it, we find ourselves in a total
wreck

Not knowing if we're coming or going confused and in a daze
why because we've fell victim to our own selfish ways
Now again, May I ask you.

IS YOUR HOUSE IN ORDER

Did you even offer to help that old lady across the street?

What about that homeless man, who asked for money, for a bite to eat?

Or did you past judgment you know try to play GOD

Remember how you felt, when that happened to you hum, now doesn't that seem odd
The nerve of them, you said who do they think they are
Have I gotten your attention yet, does this remind of anyone,
So far

I know it's hard, to be that critical of oneself
But you can do it, and so can I if we put our pride on the shelf
The time is drawing nearer, and what we think, won't be worth one quarter

At the second coming of The Christ, again I ask....

IS YOUR HOUSE IN ORDER

HIS MERCY ENDURETH 4 EVER

In a world that sometimes Is hard to cope
But for his mercy this gives us a reason to hope
That tomorrow the sun will shine again
Enabling us to find strength, that lies deep within
The restitutes of our minds, body & soul
For it is by His grace, that we are made whole
He's given us the power to bind up, and cast out the
adversary in his Holy Name.
If you don't know this by now then you have only you to
blame
Because of love, He placed himself in harm's way
Just so you and I, could see a brighter day
Not the day that tomorrow will bring
But the day that we all look forward to, listening to the angels
sing
In spite of our iniquities, transgression, and such
He laid down His life because He loves us so much
Vowing to never leave, nor forsake us never
Why you might ask... Because His Mercy Endureth 4 Ever

IT'S IN HIS WORD

It all began when He said, Let There Be Light
And it continued when He Sent Himself if by way of a virgin,
to make what went wrong, now right
He performed wonders that Sent unbelievers into rage
Some of them, were done at an early age
This caused even his Mother to question, how and why have
you done this
And He firmly replied. "I must be about My Father's Business"
Giving sight to the blind, strength to the legs of the lame
Who is this Man, they asked, Jesus is his name
With all the persecution, He prayed for them instead
Why He even fed 5000 people, with 2 fish and 5 loaves of
bread
Instructing us to instead of fighting back, to pray for them
There once was a woman, who was cleansed, just by touching
His hem
How about when He touched the water, and turned it to wine
I'm talking about JESUS, He's yours, and He's mine
To believe anyone else, could do these things, would be absurd
If you don't believe me, then read it for yourself for...

IT'S IN HIS WORD

THANK YOU GOD

For all of the mercy that you`ve shown me
How from out of the darkness, and into the light, you set
me free

All because of the love for the world, you gave
your son
Sent here on earth, to 'be the one

Who would give His life, so that we may live
So unselfishly, He loved us so, that His life He
would give

THANK YOU GOD

SHOW ME, THE WAY LORD

I'm really lost, concerning what I'm supposed to do
It's a feeling that I had so many times; haven't you
Do I go this way, or should I be still
One thing for certain, I want to do GODS WILL

Show me, the Way Lord

For I seem to always, make a mess, doing it my way
I need to hear a WORD from you what more, can I say
Just a WORD from you, will make my path straight
Father, I realize your time, is not like my time; so I'll wait
You said just ask in your Son's name, Father GOD, On Precious Lord

I need you now, for another mistake, I cannot afford
Father you know all, and see all, even before we know what
we are going to do
Speak to my heart, Sweet Jesus I need a Word from You
I really desire for my mind and my heart to be on one accord
This is my Prayer

Show Me, The Way Lord

MY WALK & MY TALK

As I gaze into the looking glass,

contemplating my future, analyzing my past

Have I been what you've called me to be?

Or am I still just trying to be me the old me

Often times I've Sensed the urgency to do GOD'S will

How is it then that I continue to fall short; deeper still?

Trial after trial, test after test you've delivered me, you

brought me thru

Who else could have such mercy no one else, only you

This gift you've blessed me with to express how I feel

I now realize it's for me to do GOD'S WILL

So many times you've spared me, saved me from myself

For there has been times, that I have put in jeopardy my

own health

To the point that my body could have been outlined with

chalk

Telling me it's time for me to line up

MY WALK & MY TALK

THRU THE FIRE

It truly amazes me, of how much one can take

The very thing that can make you laugh, can make another break

How often, have you asked yourself why me

I don't do anything; to nobody is the usual plea

We all have something, we must go thru

It's going to happen to me, and yes even you

So here is something, if I may suggest

Try to keep in mind, this is only a test

The word of GOD says, He won't put more on you than you can bare

These words I write is because I care

To offer some relief is my sincerest desire

May GOD BLESS, as you go, Through The Fire..,

THE JOURNEY

AS we travel thru this thing called life
Going in and out of the, highways and byways, tempered
with joy and strife
The winding roads that lead to where only GOD knows
But it's already written, as to where the road goes
For it's all part of elaborate plan
Designed, predestined even, and revealed to the Son of
Man
Yet, in the grand scheme of things, getting to the
Kingdom is the Ultimate Goal
The place where we all can anchor our soul
Meanwhile, as we're in route to get to this place
Much is required, as we run this race
Though the race is not for the swift, it require great
endurance
For it's not against anyone, but against your
circumstance
And how we come to adjust, to find our pace, you see
AS we travel thru life, as we make THE JOURNEY...

WALK BY FAITH/NOT BY SIGHT

The size of a mustard seed, is all we need for our faith to grow
With the understanding, the HOLY SPIRIT will provide, of those things you need to know
To lean not on thine own understanding, but on the word of GOD
Of these instructions hold them close, closer than two peas in a pod
For we never know, of the trials that we'll go thru
Yet when they're upon us, we tend to worry about what to do
In our search for resolve, we tend to struggle with wrong or right

Walk by faith/Not by Sight
A never ending struggle when we try and do it our own way
Not until all else fails, do we seek what The Word has to say
Instinctively, or call it human nature we try and make it on our own
But do we really make it? Or is it our Father who sits on the throne
Who wants us to believe in HIM, just as we believe, after day

comes the night?

Then why can't we trust in what GOD can do, if we...

WALK BY FAITH/NOT BY SIGHT

ORDER MY STEPS

Every time you make the decision to do what's right
The adversary is watching, and he won't give up without a
fight
Try as he may to deceive, confuse and distract you
From receiving GODS blessings, and the works that he has in
store for you to do

Doesn't this tell you something, or are you just to blind to see
That GOD loves you, in spite of yourself, unconditionally
He always offers us an exit, before the destruction
Because, He loves all of his children, there's no exception
All we have to do is call on him in His son, Jesus's Holy name
And from that day forward your life will never be the same
Rest, rule and abide over my life, from this day forward
So that whatever you would have me to say or do, may your
kingdom receive your reward

For I know my riches are stored up in heaven, and not here
on earth
Teach me to be as faithful as your 12 apostles, committed for
all that it was worth

Not as men pleasers, self-serving, or after lofty reps.
But for the Kingdom of God…

ORDER MY STEPS

DEAR GOD

Dear God? I really need to hear from you

You see, as I make this walk, I need your guidance, please show me what to do

I realize you have more than I, to take care of

But I truly need to hear a word from heaven up above

My utmost desire is to wholly and obediently spread your word

Most gracious Father on high I know it's not absurd

Given that I have come to share some very spiritual revelations from you

I come to you now, just as you have instructed me, too.

Since accepting your Son Jesus, it doesn't seem odd

To write this poem to you titled DEAR GOD..,

TEACH

Teach me O Lord, on what it is in your will for me to do

For I keep making mistakes, take me guide me, for my heart's desire is to follow you

Teach me Lord, for your will is how I want my life to fulfilled

Won't you, if you would in my life let your purpose be revealed?

I'm so tired of running, from what it is you want me to See, and feel

Teach me, my father so that I maybe in your perfect will

MY WILL OR THY WILL

I have some questions I'd like to ask of you

Concerning your life choices, and what you do

Do you handle them your own way, is this true?

Or do you place them in hands of our Savior

Or did you react, with an irrational behavior

Causing an even bigger situation

Because you reacted, with no hesitation

MY WILL OR THY WILL

Have you considered, just maybe, this was a time when you needed GOD?

Or does this sound ridiculous maybe even a little odd

However in hindsight, the purpose was too real

Are operating on MY WILL THY WILL...

DO YOU, KNOW HIS VOICE

Have you ever took the time to do this

That voice of reason, that cautions you, is it his

His, meaning GOD'S, speaking to your heart

Offering you a way out, before the destruction starts

Have you heard him, or did you think, it was all in your head

So you kept right on going down the wrong path instead

And it wasn't until you gotten in too deep

That you decide to listen and His face you now seek

When all you had to do, is take heed, for we all have a choice

When God is speaking to you heart...

DO YOU KNOW HIS VOICE?

LET US PRAY

What has our world come to?

Our youth are our future yet their killing one another what can we do?

LET US PRAY

Parents killing children, children killing parents, it's such a mess

We all need to get down on are knees, and with our tongues confess

LET US PRAY

For when prayers are sent up, the blessings come down

This is very much needed, in each and every town

It's becoming all the familiar, to hear on the news another tragic situation

Why because of an misunderstanding, resulting in an needless altercation

Imagine what would happen if you or I would just say

The next time when you're angry...

LET US PRAY

I'M BLESSED

When I think about all the obstacles, that I've been thru

It's only by God's grace, there has to be work for me to do

Why else would He have allowed me still be here

Even as I write these words, His presence is near

What an awesome feeling, to be in the midst of the Holy Spirit

Just thinking about Him, and I can feel it

There was a time when I was out of control, and full of stress

After all that God, has brought me thru, I'm Blessed

RAY OF HOPE

Each of us needs to hold on to the belief

That after the storm, we'll find relief

For in this life, as we press ahead, in spite of the undermining

Some may call it the dark cloud, with a silver lining

Never, giving in to the pressures, that life can bring

I refuse to lose, is the song that I sing

Yes called, even chosen to complete this walk

Even in the silent tears, I cry the Holy Spirit gives me the
words, when I talk

How else can I explain what's become apparent to me

My life is not my own, but it's God's, you See

Making it all possible for me, in this world to cope

I give him the glory, I give Him the praise, For He is my
Ray of Hope

A LESSON LEARNED

Their once was a time when I just couldn't believe

That the idea, of my way would end, I just couldn't conceive

A LESSON LEARNED
How foolish was I, to be so full of myself

Never even realizing, that I had placed my blessings on the shelf

A LESSON LEARNED
Time after time, mistake after mistake, I just couldn't discern

But then I found JESUS, by his grace and mercy this is now

A LESSON LEARNED

I'M STILL STANDING

I've been in the trenches for a mighty long time
Pressing on, in spite of my adversities, when there is no
riddle nor rhyme
For the battle's not mine, for it's the Lord
He, whom has given me strength, as my reward
Especially during those times, when I was lost, and in
despair
My faith never wavered, for He was always there
As my rock, my strength, yes even my strong tower
With the patience of job, I stand, even in the eleventh
hour
For it's by grace and mercy, that HE saves
I'm still standing, on HIS word for the rest of my days
He restores my soul, in a world that's so demanding
Surely you can see why,
I'm Still Standing..

NOWHERE ELSE TO RUN

I had a "call" last night, but it wasn't by phone

It was from my "FATHER" telling me you're not alone

Times may be rough, particularly going the last mile

But he implored to me, my son trouble only last for awhile

Come to me He stated, I'll make you burdens light

For in me you'll find peace, so you can rest thru the night

Tomorrow will come, as last night will be done

Come to me my child, for you have

Nowhere Else to Run

THE HOLY SPIRIT

Today my heart is heavy, and I didn't know what to do

Then I felt your "Presence" telling me, to call on you

For in my darkest moments, feeling down trodden, and in despair

I can always call on you, for you will always be there

Regardless of the problem, big or small

In you I can rely on, to see me thru it all

No matter the race, creed, or gender it has nothing to do with it

He's there for all of us, For He is

The Holy Spirit

NOW IS THE TIME

After all you've been thru, you must realize Now is the Time

You can't hesitate nor delay,

What I have in Store for you is here and now yes today"

Now Is The Time There so much work to be done

 I need you my son, you are The One

To spread my word, throughout the land

Those who have ears listen, for the Kingdom of God is at Hand

Now Is the Time

Come one, come all, take heed to my word for it's you whom I call

Beckoning for you to receive this blessing, here today

For thru his son Jesus is the only way

Although this message is done in a rhyme

Take it seriously for-

Now Is The TIME!

FOR YOU

There' nothing that I wouldn't do for you

Just to see a smile on your face would be like a dream come true.

Whateveryour heart desire

I'd try and never tire

You see it really doesn't matter what you ask of me to do

I'll do it with a smile - just for you

'Inspirational Poetry'

INSPIRATIONS

T. Oscar Whaley

Inspirations

Vol.3

AS A REMINDER

Maybe your day was too busy to say

Hello, how are you, or how was your day

It could be that you just simply forgot
But I love you anyway, whether you say it
or not

Or there may be something, I could've
done
To let you know, you're the only one

So from now on, I'll be a little kinder
This is for you, As a Reminder...

IF I FAIL

If I fail to show you, how much I care

Then let me remind you, I'm always there

When I can't be there, when you call on me

Trust and believe, in my heart you'll always be

I should be more attentive, understanding of what
you need

Just know, I won't stop trying, until I succeed

I'll be right there, in times of trouble

With the utmost urgency, I'll be there on the
double

Anything to please you, as you can tell

To make it up to you, If I fail

STILL IN LOVE

The road has been rough, troubles have been many
Though I`ve searched the world over, I haven't
found any

That could bring me joy, the way that you do
You are as refreshing, as the morning dew

As it covers the fresh cut lawn

One of the gifts we receive, after the dawn

Of course it makes, for all the reason
To be still in love, in any season...

FROM THE START

There's a feeling that came over me today
Where it came from, I cannot say

All I know is since then, not a lonely day
have I spent-
It's how I know, you are heaven sent

Love has been placed, upon my heart

There's emptiness I f eel when we're apart

When we're together, it's like life imitates
art
I've always known this, From the Start

These words are written from the bottom of
my heart
I fell In Love with you right,

From the Start...

MISUNDERSTOOD

It's some feeling, to know of you, there is
always doubt

By all you encounter, it appears to be no
`way out

No matter what you say, or what you do
There always is someone, accusing you

Your efforts to try, and show in you,
`there is some humility?

But time and again, they question your
ability

The word around town is you are no good
when reality the problem is you're
Misunderstood...

DID YOU EVER

As you come closer to achieving success

Something always happens, trying to make you regress

The problem is there is always someone willing
to see you fail

Over all these obstacles, you can still prevail

Always remember, they're always out there
trying to be clever

Tell me have you considered these things

Did You Ever...

DO YOU KNOW

What is life, but a moment in time?

To be enjoyed to the fullest, it's yours it's mine

Make the best of it, for we never know
For it's here today and gone tomorrow

We all desire, basically the same dream

To be happy, a chance to taste the cream

That rises to the top that accompanies success

All things are possible, when you give it your best

In all of us, we have a destiny, in which we must
follow

Of this I'm sure, now tell me do you know...

COME TOO FAR

To turn back now, not an option

From this day forward, to the wind I throw caution

As I know, what I am destined to be

A man with a purpose, the essence of me

Never again will I feed into the doubts, and
misconceptions

For I know my self -worth, I have a sense of
direction

It's doesn't matter, the obstacles, devices or who
they are

There's no turning back now, I've

COME TOO FAR

STEP OUTSIDE OF YOURSELF

Step outside of yourself, what will you see
It's an invaluable act, of humility

This requires one, to truly humble oneself

To take a look, at who you are, do it now or else

The end result may be more than you think
For the change can happen, quicker than the eye
can blink

You really must do this, in order to believe
What you see, you can change, only after you
conceive

Once on the outside, there's a different point of
view
Giving yourself a chance to see a healthy
perspective of you

In doing so, you can place all your worries on the shelf
But f first you must, Step Outside of Yourself ...

DEEPER STILL

When you look at what's on the surface, it's not

always what it appears to be

Look a little deeper, do you like what you see

There's always a chance, it could be as you suspect

Often times, you then view it, in retrospect

So approach the situation, with eyes wide open if
you will

There's always more to it, if you look Deeper Still...

IT'S YOUR TURN

You believe that things will never be in your favor

Will there ever be, a moment that you savior

`Your reason for doubt is fair, but when will you learn

To finally stop, and believe that now,
It's your Turn

Maybe it hurts, when you reflect

On the bad times, filled with neglect

So I tell you again, I hope you can discern

The time has come; it's your turn...

IS ANYTHING FOR CERTAIN

How do you know, what tomorrow will bring

I often ask this question, it's the song I sing

Why does the bird fly, so high in the sky?

What makes you happy, what brought that tear to

your eye?

Is there really, such a thing as true love?

This can only be answered, from heaven up above

The sun is shining brightly; I think I'll draw back
my curtain

As I look out my window, I ask myself
Is anything for Certain..?

WHERE DO WE GO

It all started out so good
We were both in transition, this was understood

WHERE DO WE GO

There the ups & downs, of life's pit falls
You and I together, preserving thru it all

WHERE DO WE GO

Spiritually connected, clearly with an divine intent
How can we not see, the purpose is Heaven sent

WHERE DO WE GO

With patience, obedience, and tempered with Love
The union will be complete, ordained from Heaven,
Up Above

THE FORGIVEN HEART

In this life we have our trials and tribulations

Yet there is comfort in knowing its but for a while,
in this we can have celebrations

Though it may appear, that you're caught in a
tornadoes funnel

Rest assure, for there is a light, at the end of tunnel

For this all comes about, but you must first make start

And this all begins, with

The Forgiven Heart

IF I KNEW

How does one come to realize?
Just how to love unconditionally come closer,
take a look, do you see it in my eyes
Perhaps it was when I held your hand
And told you, by far you're not alone in this
land
A place where nobody seems to really care
Come, sit right here, relax, may
I run my fingers, thru your hair
With each passing moment, as I become
better acquainted with you
Am I any closer to your heart, just what will
it take-

    IF I KNEW...

FIRST OF, ALL

Let me start by saying,
You are all I think of

My mind goes in a daze, like
When you gaze, up at the stars in the heavens
above

I knew you were special, in each and every way

It's just as natural, as night turns to day

(Picture if you will, the summer, as it turns to fall

When I think of you, that's
What I see First of All...

REMEMBER

Do you remember when we first met?

It was like heaven's gate opened up, how could
I forget?

Although it's been quite a while, since I've
seen you

I can't get you off my mind, what am I to do

Of course I realize, you've gone on with your
life

But not long ago, you were almost my wife

My how things change, I hope you're doing
fine
I still have fond memories, of when you were mine.

THAT'S HOW LIFE GOES

Here's something I'm sure you can relate to

In life, you never know, just what you'll go thru

How often have you asked, yourself this question

When it has to do with, your life, everyone has a suggestion

Most of the time, their own affairs aren't even straight

So think before you react, for tomorrow will be too late

But this is not news, for everyone knows

Take it in stride because That's How Life Goes...

ONCE AGAIN

On my own, once again why me

All I ever wanted was someone to love me, for me

I know I've made mistakes, but I'm only human

You told me, you loved me
So what are you doing?

I thought this time was forever how wrong I was

Did you really mean it, or was it just because

If I could turn back the hands of time

I surely would, it reminds of the days when you
were mine

WHILEST I'M ALONE

Have you ever considered, how the mind retains so much

Or why is that, you can have pleasure or pain from the slightest touch

WHILEST I'M ALONE

I've contemplated these thoughts, as my life takes on yet another turn
Asking myself, over and over again, when will I learn?

WHILEST I'M ALONE

Here's the opportunity, to listen to see, to face the facts
Has this been coincidental, or because of my acts
Why didn't I learn, after going in the zone?
This is what I think about

WHILEST I'M ALONE

WHAT I HEARD

They say a picture is worth a thousand words

But, the few times that we've talked it's
What you didn't' say, that I heard.

Strong and wise, a beautiful black queen

I can see GOD has a plan for you, you know what I
mean?

I heard a lot of talk around here, and it's quite
absurd

But's it's more of -what they don't say, is

WHAT I HEARD

THE ONE

That's who I am can't you see I'm your MAN!

Can I make you happy? Yes I can

Not just the average Joe, a cut above the
rest, or did you know

I'm able to change, your gray skies to blue

All that and more, if you allow me too

They call me Tracy Oscar, T. O.
THE ONE

There will never be another like
me, not anyone

For all in all it's by God's Grace

I wrote this poem, but I can also express it
face to face

How many times, before you realize

I know you can see it, when you look into my
eyes

I'm serious man, but I also like to have fun

But I am definitely serious when I tell you I'm

THE ONE...

About The Author

T. Oscar Whaley "Tracy" Is A Native Of Dayton Ohio, Ordained Minister, Single Father, Author Of Life Skills For Men "Single Male Parent" Perspective & Teen Pregnancy "Addressing The Counterpart" Both Unpublished. Discovering The Gift Of Poetry Came When I Wrote A Poem For The Life Skills Program; From There They Just Began To Flow Naturally From Me.

I Am Thankful For The Blessing To Have My First Book Published. I Call It A Blessing By The Way I Came To Be Published. The Opportunity To Share With A Total Stranger, Led To My Introduction To Pure Thoughts Publishing.

Grateful For The People Who Were Placed In The Path Of My Journey, Of Which I Knew Not, Yet Here Was An

Opportunity To Share The Gift Of Poetry Of Which I Now Share With You.

I Titled Them "Hues Of A Rainbow" As They Speak To Spirituality "God Inspired", Reflection Of "The Spirit" As Well As Circumstances Pertaining To Life "Inspirations", Along With Affairs Of Heart "Hues Of A Rainbow"; For Each Title I See Each Color Representing, The Ebbs &Flows Of Life.

My Passion For Poetry Affords Me The Chance By Way Of Expression Of Words Formed Together To Share With Everyone; May You Find The End Of Your Rainbow Abound In Blessings.

www.ingramcontent.com/pod-product-compliance
Lightning Source LLC
Chambersburg PA
CBHW021241090426
42740CB00006B/630